BLACK DOG MUSIC LIBRARY

Gregorian Chant and Polyphony

BLACK DOG MUSIC LIBRARY

Gregorian Chant and Polyphony

Jerusalem
Holy Week
Easter
Pentecost
Psalm for the Office of Advent
Mass of Advent

*Performed by the Monastic Choir of l'Abbaye du Bec-Hellouin
under the direction of Brother Philibert Zobel*

TEXT BY DAVID FOIL

BLACK DOG & LEVENTHAL PUBLISHERS
NEW YORK

Published by
Black Dog & Leventhal Publishers Inc.
151 West 19th Street
New York, NY 10011

Distributed by
Workman Publishing Company
708 Broadway
New York, NY 10003

Designed by Martin Lubin and Allison Russo

Special thanks to Judith Dupré

Book manufactured in Hong Kong

ISBN: 1-884822-41-X

FOREWORD

Gregorian chant is the oldest form of notated music in the Western world yet its worldwide popularity and following have never been greater than they are today. This musical form and tradition affirm beauty, mystery, faith, and timelessness. Its message is a fundamental and simple one that has inspired devotion for nearly two millennia.

This book explains the monastic world and the liturgy expressed in the chants. In this volume you will be able to better understand the significance, the meaning, and the message of these works; and you can enjoy and listen to the music as you read.

Play the compact disc included on the inside front cover of this book and follow along with the commentary and analysis. Please note that the track numbers of the relevant musical passages are noted for your convenience.

Enjoy this book and enjoy the music.

Gregorian Chant

In 1993 and 1994, a seismic pop trend shook the world of classical music. It carried all the trappings of a musical blockbuster—platinum-selling CDs and tapes, bootleg versions both crude and sublime, concert tours, books, and videos. It provoked the kind of harrumphing commentary from the musical establishment that is heard whenever serious music achieves popular success and it touched off a controversy far greater than the usual tempest in a teapot such as the debate about whether Baroque and Classical music should be played on original instruments. It wasn't a multimedia extravaganza like "The Three Tenors" concerts. The trend couldn't even be described as new.

Kneeling Monk
by Edouard Manet

It was, of all things, a passion for Gregorian chant—Western civilization's oldest known body of notated music. Gregorian chant had taken the world by storm as a result of EMI Classics' shrewdly marketed rerelease of recordings made in Spain twenty years earlier by an obscure group of Benedictine monks. In the United States, Angel/EMI Classics packaged the recording with an arresting cover painting: a Magritte-like image of praying monks suspended in front of a blue sky. The catchy one-word title, *Chant,* also drove the marketing effort, one that cannily balanced the reverent nature of Gregorian chant with the growing public demand for the music. Some music critics and historians complained that the recordings lacked clarity, musical distinction, and the proper historical style of performance, and insisted that other recordings presented a much purer realization of Gregorian chant. Perhaps the Benedictine monks of the Spanish monastery of Santo Domingo de Silos—the reluctant stars of this phenomenon—captured the public's imagination because they weren't preoccupied with musicological concerns. When all the window-dressing was swept away, what spoke to the audience was the artless conviction of the monks' singing. The popularity of these recordings—*Chant* in the United States and *Canto Gregoriano* in Europe—transcended cultures, and they outsold many pop recordings. Despite its intrinsic connection to Roman Catholicism, Gregorian chant became a favorite of people who professed no religious belief, embraced no church, and did not pray in the traditional sense. Chant had been transformed into a New Age easy-listening hit.

The pop trendiness of Gregorian chant has precedent: In the 1960s, as rock music struggled to achieve some kind of profundity, young listeners explored anything that sounded "heavy"—unusual and apart from mundane experience. To these listeners, Gregorian chant had the same kind of timeless "otherness" as the pungent delicacy of Ravi Shankar's sitar music and held out the appeal of Eastern mysticism, co-opted by so many rock stars. Gregorian chant seemed to have a purity of purpose, stripped of affectation or decadence. The simple, inimitable sound of chant was mesmerizing; recordings of it gained cult favor (much as did Walt Disney's film *Fantasia*) with those who took drugs in an effort to heighten their consciousness.

It might be argued that the newfound popularity of Gregorian chant in the 1990s signaled a renewed yearning for spirituality or that its rediscovery was nothing more than a fad, a way for a fickle audience to try on

Trappist monks at prayer at the Abbaye Soligny de la Trappe founded in 530.

the trappings of faith without engaging in its substance or meeting its stark challenges. In fact, many Roman Catholics were appalled by the emergence of Gregorian chant into the popular culture. As they saw it, a venerable form of worship had been swept into a secular context that ignored the literal meaning of the texts and their profoundly important role in worship. In its original context, chanting was not necessarily meant to comfort and reassure. Unswerving devotion and selflessness were demanded of the clergy by this prayerful and physically challenging endeavor.

As a century of unimaginable progress—and equally unimaginable horror—draws to a close, we are witnessing a burst of orthodoxy in every religion. Millions are swooning to the simple, unadorned sound of ancient music that was designed only to fulfill a monk's daily duty to pray humbly and praise God.

What, then, is the secret of the modern success of Gregorian chant? Perhaps simply that it sounds like nothing else. The Latin texts and spare, ethereal musical line are so far removed from the ordinary elements of our daily lives that they entrance us, whether or not we understand the meaning of the words. Gregorian chant reflects the almost magical power of chanting recognized and used by all religions. The music in this collection goes beyond Gregorian chant into the comparatively modern sound-world of polyphony, but the mystique remains the same.

What Is Gregorian Chant?

Gregorian chant is the foundation of all liturgical music in the Western Christian tradition. In our time, the term *Gregorian chant* broadly refers to the official chant of the Roman Catholic Church—the ritual melody that prevailed in the monolithic Western Christian church before the upheavals that led to the Reformation. The term *Gregorian chant* can be misleading; the label was applied when the chants were notated and collected for posterity, long after they had been composed. What we call Gregorian chant may be most accurately called plainchant, or plainsong, taken from the Latin term *cantus planus*.

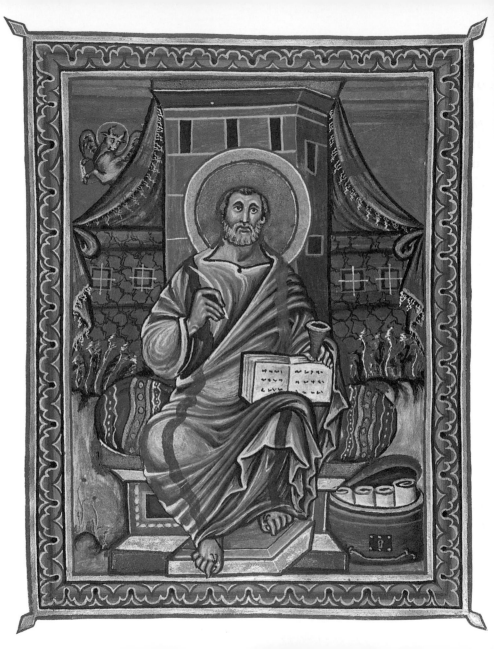

Plainchant consists of a single musical line, sung without accompaniment or rhythm. It has its own distinctive musical notation, which does not divide the musical line into bars, or measures. Those characteristics distinguish *cantus planus* from *cantus figuratus* ("figured song," suggesting an embellished musical line with some sort of accompaniment) and *cantus mensuratus* ("measured song," suggesting the presence of rhythm). The lack of rhythm in plainchant allows the music to capture the free patterns of speech, instead of conforming to the meter of poetry. Plainchant was the perfect musical format for prayers, meditations, and psalms.

The psalms of the Old Testament were a primary source of chant texts, as were passages from the historical books of the Old Testament. Nonbiblical poetic texts, particularly hymns, were also set to chant. In its earliest years, the Church fought the inclusion of secular text, considering it an affront to the purity and the divine source of the liturgy. It even banned the use of hymns in the liturgy in an edict of the fourth-century Council of Laodicea, as well as in successive councils for the next three hundred years. However, the practice flourished, particularly in France, and gained a powerful spokesman in St. Benedict (480–547), who founded the Benedictine monastic order. The hymnal adopted by the Roman Catholic Church in the tenth or eleventh century was a Benedictine hymnal.

Some form of chant is a primary feature of most ancient ceremonies of Eastern and Western worship. Tibetan monks have their own distinctive vocal style. In the Hindu faith, a mantra (a word repeated over and over, often on musical tones) can have the same effect as chant—mantra itself means "mystical repetition," or "a sound that makes one see." Most Native American ceremonies feature chanting, often accompanied by drumming.

Saint Luke the Evangelist, *manuscript page from the* **Utrecht Psalter,** *France, 845-882.*

Within Christianity, the development of chant had broad implications that were realized in different ways after the schism occurred between the Eastern and Western churches. Before the schism—in which the Western church followed the Roman pope and the Eastern church the patriarch of Constantinople—Jerusalem, Antioch, Rome, and Constantinople were the centers of activity in the Holy Roman Empire. The practices followed in the churches in these cities had the greatest influence on the development of

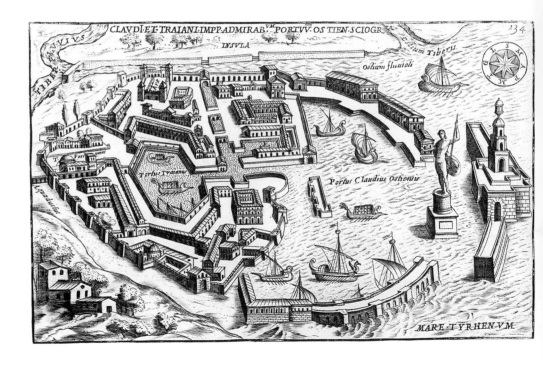

Early map of the city of Rome

Pope Gregory I receiving inspiration from the Holy Spirit depicted in a thirteenth-century miniature.

Christian chant in the latter period of the empire. The rise of Constantinople as the eastern capital of the Holy Roman Empire led to the creation of a separate tradition of chant in the Eastern Orthodox Church. Plainchant is a result of the musical traditions evolved by the Western church, specifically in Rome.

Who composed these chants? There are thousands of them, collected over the centuries, most the result of setting down existing oral traditions. The most common chants were the first ones recorded. There was no school of composers of chant, as there would be for later church music. Chant evolved as it came into contact with different societies and changes in the liturgy.

The term *Gregorian* refers to the sixth-century Roman Catholic Pope Gregory I (c. 540–604) who was invested in 590. By all accounts a remarkable man, Pope Gregory I was known as Gregory the Great and was later elevated to sainthood. He was involved in the development and arrangement of the liturgy, and for centuries it was assumed that the collected body of Roman Catholic plainchant was the result of his innovations. Medieval icons depict the Holy Father in just such a moment of creation. As a dove whispers in his

Holy Roman Emperor
Charlemagne *by Albrecht
Durer, ca. 1512*

ear, a scribe records the musical inspiration. The early teachings of the Church supported this perception.

Modern scholarship has cast serious doubt on Gregory I's responsibility for the development of plainchant; many of the elements of the music we know as Gregorian chant were created after his reign. The oldest surviving manuscripts of Gregorian chant date from the eleventh and twelfth centuries —four hundred years after Gregory I's death—and their origins can be traced only to the eighth century.

Yet some credit is due him. It is possible that the development of Roman Catholic plainchant resulted from Gregory I's highly specific ideas about the liturgy. Willi Apel, in his definitive study *Gregorian Chant*, notes that Gregory I's considerable writings do not suggest that he was especially interested in chant or even sympathetic to its demands. He had stern words for those who placed too much emphasis on musical values or a good voice when selecting a deacon. He ordered that all chant be sung by lower-level clerics, with the exception of the Gospel. Gregory I seems to have been involved in bringing order to the liturgy and in specifying a clear-cut role within it for chant. Whether these were his efforts or those of subordinates carrying out his wishes, Gregory I had a powerful impact on succeeding generations. While the term *Gregorian chant* is not entirely factual, it does give plainchant a general historical context.

Much of the development of Gregorian chant took place in the eighth and ninth centuries in northern France and Germany. During the reign of the Holy Roman Emperor Charlemagne, a period known as the Carolingian Renaissance, a concerted though fruitless effort was made to keep Roman chant from becoming corrupted by local practices. Soon the idiosyncrasies of regional chant blended with the Roman, expanding the nature and practice of plainchant.

The Texts

The message of the sacred texts is the foundation of chant. To the listener who has no connection with Christianity, the texts might seem redundant and quite separate from the musical effect of Gregorian chant. But this is music with a specific purpose—to enhance the impact of the liturgy. The musical structure and character of Gregorian chant are the result of an effort to make the message of the texts clear.

The subject of the text is the core of the Christian faith, praising God and praying for forgiveness and deliverance through the sacrificial life, death, and resurrection to eternal life of Jesus Christ. It is an essentially simple message but one from which believers draw endless spiritual sustenance. The monks for whom Gregorian chant was devised were dedicated to prayer and to performing good works on behalf of mankind. The Mass and the Divine Office of the liturgy consumed much of their daily lives.

Chant can be heard in both the Mass and the Divine Office of the Roman Catholic Church's liturgy. The Mass is the church's most solemn service, the foundation of worship that observes and mystically re-creates the transformation first experienced at the Last Supper of Jesus Christ. The Mass has two parts, the Proper and the Ordinary (sometimes called the Common). A High Mass is sung, and a Low Mass is spoken; chant is sung only at a High Mass.

The Ordinary, the core of the Mass, remains constant, while the Proper changes. The five principal sections of the Mass are the *Kyrie* ("Lord have

Doorway of the thirteenth-century monastery of Moutiers-Saint-Jean, France.

mercy"); the *Gloria* ("Glory be to God in the highest"); the *Credo* ("I believe"); the *Sanctus* ("Holy, holy, holy"); and the *Agnus Dei* ("O Lamb of God"). The Mass concludes with the instruction *"Ite, missa est congregatio"* ("Depart, the congregation is dismissed").

Manuscript illumination

The Proper includes texts and chants that change daily with the liturgical calendar. The Proper alternates with the Ordinary, and it opens the Mass with an introductory section called the Introit. Following the *Gloria* of the Ordinary, the Gradual is heard, in which psalms or verses are sung, followed by responses. A hymn of praise, the Alleluia, follows, except during Lent and other significant periods, when the Tract (in which psalms are sung without responses) is sung in its place. After the *Credo* comes the

Offertory, during which gifts of bread and wine are placed on the altar in preparation for Communion. The *Sanctus* and the *Agnus Dei* of the Ordinary are then heard. The Mass reaches its peak in the Communion, in which the bread and wine are mystically transformed into the body and blood of Christ; the Communion section of the High Mass is sung after the distribution of the bread and wine.

The Divine Office includes the services of daily hours made up of psalms, canticles, antiphons, responsories, hymns, lessons, and prayers. These services structure the daily rituals of monastic life. There are eight services in the Office—Matins, sung in the morning before dawn; Lauds, sung immediately after Matins; Prime, sung around six a.m.; Terce, sung around nine a.m.; Sext, sung around noon; None, sung around three p.m.; Vespers, sung at sunset; and Compline, sung before retiring for the night. The Mass fits into this schedule variously: On ordinary weekdays, it follows Sext; on fast days, it follows None; otherwise, it is heard after Terce.

The Music

The desire to codify and notate Gregorian chant is the reason we have our Western system of musical notation. It was literally invented for the writing down of Gregorian chant. The form of musical notation we use today has developed considerably over the past thousand years. The earliest written music uses a system of figures called neumes (from the Greek word *neuma*, meaning "gesture" or "sign").

At first, this notation involved nothing more than accents over a horizontal line to indicate the rise and fall of musical pitch accompanying the

Portrait of a Monk
by G. Boccati

text. Eventually neumes came to represent exact musical pitches on a staff of bar lines. In plainchant four bar lines are used instead of the five employed in other music. By the way they were figured, neumes also indicated the duration of tones. Plainchant melodies do not have the symmetry of song because they do not conform to a rhythmic structure. They do have three degrees of complexity—the syllabic, in which each syllable has a corresponding note; the neumatic, in which small phrases of notes (as few as two, as many as fifteen) accompany each syllable; and the melismatic, in which the melody expands into a layered phrase on a single syllable. As an illustration, consider the word *Amen*, which concludes many hymns. In most instances it is sung simply on two notes, one for each syllable—that is a syllabic treatment. In a neumatic treatment, each syllable would be expanded by adding a group of notes per syllable: *Amen* is sung in a rise-and-fall manner: ah-ah-ah-ah-me-eh-eh-eh-en. Melismatic treatment is akin to coloratura singing in opera or the improvisatory rides taken by jazz and blues singers. On a single syllable, a florid musical line is created, sometimes with dozens of notes. Imagine *Amen* sung by a coloratura soprano with dazzling runs up and down the scale, all on the first syllable—that is melismatic writing. Syllabic, neumatic, and melismatic expression heightened the impact of certain key words and phrases. While Gregorian chant is essentially simple music, meant to illuminate the texts as reverently and as vividly as possible, these techniques bring an artful interpretive finesse to a utilitarian format. For many listeners, the medium of Gregorian chant is the message.

The Legacy of Gregorian Chant

As music itself began to change, the music in the church changed to accommodate the liturgy. The arrival of polyphony altered the nature of church music forever. Polyphony is a striking departure from the pure, unadorned line of Gregorian chant, which is called monophony, meaning "one sound.". Polyphony, meaning "many sounds," describes music in which several lines of individual design are heard simultaneously and more or less equally. It differs from homophony, in which a single voice might lead, to the accompaniment (often in chords) of other lines that are identical in design and rhythm. Polyphony flourished in the Renaissance and

reached its zenith in the late Baroque period in the formal music of Johann Sebastian Bach. During the Council of Trent, held between 1545 and 1563, the church sought to clarify the role of music in its rituals. The intention was to remove certain elements—embellishments known as tropes and sequences—that were believed to dilute the purity of the liturgy. The "threat" of decorative music was taken so seriously that at one point the council considered banning all music but plainchant from the liturgy. The final edict commanded that liturgical music be uplifting and called for the removal of all "impure or lascivious" influences. Texts were to be clearly sung or spoken, and the Mass was to be celebrated in Latin.

Though Gregorian chant continued to be employed, particularly by Benedictine monks, its purity became compromised over the years. The

Interior of twelfth-century Church of the Madeleine in Vézelay, France

strict adherence to long-held practices in the singing of chant slackened, and the experience of singing other kinds of music inevitably affected the way monks approached Gregorian chant. New developments in music allowed for more latitude in interpretation and performance; some chant was performed with rhythmic meter and instrumental accompaniment.

Gregorian chant had always had a strong tradition in France, and a modern movement to restore the practice of Gregorian chant had its beginnings there in the nineteenth century, culminating in the publication of critical editions of chant by the Benedictine abbey of Saint-Pierre de Solesmes in 1883. This modern scholarship on Gregorian chant led to its translation into a modern musical language. Decades of debate were involved in the quest for papal acceptance of a standard modern text for plainchant for use in the church. In 1903 Pope Pius X officially recognized plainchant as the highest and purest form of liturgical music, praising the work of the monks of Solesmes in restoring its integrity. The following year an official edition of plainchant was authorized by the Vatican. It was published in several volumes over the next decade, amid argument and considerable scholarly rancor between groups of academics. A German group of scholars in Gregorian chant called the Cecilian Movement was influential throughout Europe and the Americas, and its work was often at odds with that of the Solesmes school. The Vatican commission that oversaw the publication awarded the privilege of editing to the monks of Solesmes, but disagreements led to the loss of that privilege. Secular scholarship has continued through the twentieth century, adding enormously to the body of knowledge about plainchant.

Crucifixion. *Cover of the* Lindau Gospels *from the workshop of Charles the Bald, c. 875.*

After the Council of Trent, the next dramatic changes in the musical policies of the Roman Catholic Church came four hundred years later, between 1962 and 1965, at the Second Vatican Council. Among Vatican II's many reforms, one of the most controversial was the replacement of Latin in the Mass with the vernacular of the communicants. The essential sound of

Pope John XXIII signing a papal bull proclaiming that the Second Vatican Council will be held in 1962.

the Roman Catholic ritual was lost in the process, to the despair of many traditional Catholics. Perhaps the contemporary popularity of Gregorian chant can be linked to their desire to hear the timeless, elevated sounds of the liturgy in Latin once again.

Gregorian Chant and Polyphony Today

In its early form, with the original Latin texts, Gregorian chant is a striking archaic presence in modern spiritual life. Music in the Roman Catholic Church was revolutionized by the Second Vatican Council's liberal reforms, leading to the studied informality of such innovations as "guitar masses." In the 1960s, especially in the United States, an emphasis

Cloisters of Saint-Trophisme, Arles, France. Eleventh century.

on social activism and accessible worship provided even greater distance from the formidable voice of Gregorian chant. That accessibility began to pale for many Roman Catholics, and the conservative turn the church has taken under Pope John Paul II has marked a return to traditional elements in worship.

It may seem odd, then, that Gregorian chant has flourished in the latter half of this century primarily as a show-business phenomenon, capped by the success of the *Chant* album. It is still practiced in monastic life, especially in Benedictine monasteries which have sought valiantly to preserve it.

Since it became a conscious art form in the Renaissance, Western music has resonated with the sound of Gregorian chant. It can be heard

most tellingly in the setting of words—notably in an operatic recitative or the verse of a song—and in the free expression of words in music. In the nineteenth and twentieth centuries composers borrowed the sound of chant to create special effects in concert music. Unlike other forms of liturgical music, chant does not transfer comfortably to the concert hall, though there have been efforts to perform it there. It has its greatest impact when it is sung in the resonant space of a church, where the unaccompanied musical line achieves a genuine, piercing eloquence.

Le Clerc inv
et fecit

The Recordings

These recordings of Gregorian chant and polyphony are unusual in that women as well as men are heard singing. For centuries women were enjoined from singing in church, the result of the teachings of St. Paul who believed women in church should be silent. In the religious life, there were exceptions to this rule, most notably in the efforts of the multitalented twelfth-century German nun and mystic Hildegard von Bingen, who rejected the restricted nature of prevailing liturgical music and wrote her own to accommodate the voices of her sister nuns.

For the most part, though, liturgical music was the domain of men. As music grew more complex in the age of polyphony, calling for greater range from singers, composers began to write harmonies that were richer and denser, requiring voices in the soprano and alto registers. In the Renaissance the church endorsed and benefited from the creation of *castrati* singers, a barbaric practice in which prepubescent boys were castrated to prevent their voices from changing when they matured. Though this practice lost its popularity with secular audiences in the eighteenth century, the church continued to use *castrati* singers. The last of them, Alessandro Moreschi, sang in the Sistine Chapel Choir in Rome and, as an old man, made recordings in the first decade of the twentieth century. Women's voices began to figure prominently in Roman Catholic church choirs in the twentieth century.

This recording is structured to give the listener insight into changes in the liturgy over the course of the church year. The liturgical calendar is built around a cycle of feasts and commemorations.

"Holy Mother Church is conscious that she must celebrate the saving work of her divine Spouse by devoutly recalling it on certain days throughout the course of the year," stated the edict of the Second Vatican Council. "Every week on the day which she has called the Lord's day, she keeps the memory of His resurrection. In the supreme solemnity of Easter, she also makes an annual commemoration of his resurrection, along with the Lord's blessed passion. Within the cycle of a year, moreover, she unfolds the whole

City of Jerusalem with Temple of Solomon in foreground.

mystery of Christ, not only from His incarnation and birth until His ascension, but also as reflected in the day of Pentecost, and the expectation of a blessed, hoped-for return of the Lord."

The first four chants heard here are grouped under the title *"Jerusalem"* and use the image of that holy city to represent the edifice of the church and the spiritual community of the faithful. The first, *"Urbs Jerusalem"* (Band No. 1), is a vesper hymn for the consecration of the church. The second and third—"*Da pacem*" (Band No. 2) and "*Laetatus sum*" (Band No. 3)—offer an Introit and a Gradual for the twenty-fourth Sunday of the year. The final, joyous "*Ecce quam bonum*" (Band No. 4) is a Gradual for the twenty-seventh Sunday of the year.

Holy Week precedes Easter, the annual celebration of the resurrection of Christ. Beginning with Palm Sunday and concluding with Holy Saturday, Holy Week offers the most dramatic and meaningful services of the liturgical year. The humbling hymn "*Ubi caritas*" (Band No. 5) is to be sung in the Holy Thursday service—the beginning of the three-day period known as the Easter Triduum—during the ceremonial washing of feet. The other three chants heard here figure in the commemoration of the Triduum. "*Ecce vidimus sum*" (Band No. 6) is sung as a responsory during Matins on Holy Thursday. The "*Lamentation*" (Band No. 7) is heard during Matins on Good Friday. The responsory "*Ecce quomodo*" (Band No. 8) is heard in Matins for Holy Saturday, the concluding day of the Easter Triduum.

Easter is the most significant celebration of the church year because it commemorates the resurrection of Jesus Christ on the third day after his death, commemorated on Good Friday. It is the fundamental miracle of the Christian faith, and the Easter celebration continues well past Easter Sunday, through the fifty days leading to Pentecost. The "*Haec dies*" (Band No. 9) is sung as a Gradual on the Tuesday after Easter Sunday. The famous text "*Victimae paschali laudes*" (Band No. 10) is a sequence sung in the Easter Mass.

Pentecost has special meaning for Christians, as it commemorates the descent of the Holy Spirit on Christ's Apostles. It signifies the beginning of

Nativity *by Silvestro dei Gherarducci. Leaf from a Gradual made in the fourteenth century at the monastery of Santa Maria degli Angeli, Florence.*

UER
NATE
EST
NOB'

Et Filius datus e no

bis cuius imperium

the active work of the church in spreading its message and also celebrates the end of the Easter season. In the service for the Vigil of Pentecost—when the faithful await the arrival of the Holy Spirit—"*Caritas dei*" (Band No. 11) is sung as an Introit. Two versions of the classic Pentecost text "*Veni sancte Spiritus*" ("Come, Holy Spirit") (Band Nos. 12 and 13) are heard—the first, with an Alleluia section, from the Pentecost Mass, and the second as a sequence from that Mass.

Advent is the most joyous time of the Christian year; it anticipates the birth of Christ, commemorated on Christmas Day. The choice of music in this recording expands beyond both Gregorian chant and Catholicism: The first selection, drawn from the Evening Office, is the French setting of Psalm 101 ("*O Dieu sauveur*") (Band No. 14) and the work of the sixteenth-century French composer Claude Goudimel, who converted to Protestantism and died with the Huguenots in the St. Bartholomew's Day Massacre in 1572. Another French setting, of Psalm 121 ("*O ma joie*"), is drawn from the Jerusalem Bible. From the Office for the Advent season come the hymn "*Conditor aime siderum*" (Band No. 15); "*Jerusalem*" (Band No. 16), an antiphon for the third Sunday in Advent; a French setting, "*Aspiciens a longe*" (Band No. 17), used as a responsory during the procession for the first Sunday in Advent; "*Ecce Nomen Domini*" (Band No. 18), an antiphon sung to the "*Magnificat*," also on the first Sunday in Advent; the "*Magnificat*" itself, and the "*Alma redemptoris mater*" (Band No. 19), sung as an antiphon to honor the Virgin Mary during the Advent season.

Finally we come to the Advent Mass. Included are a series of chants from the first Sunday in Advent—the Introit "*Ad te levavi*" (Band No. 20), a Gradual "*Universi*" (Band No. 22), and an "*Alleluia*" (Band No. 23). The "*Kyrie eleison*" (Band No. 21) and the "*Sanctus*" are sections of the Mass itself. The "*Préface*" (Band No. 24) is a prelude for the Advent season, and the "*Dicite pusillanimes*" (Band No. 25) is sung during communion on the third Sunday of Advent. The "*Notre Père*" ("Our Father") (band No. 26) is the central prayer of the Christian faith, heard here in a richly polyphonic setting by the Russian composer Nikolai Rimsky-Korsakov.

The Monastic Choir of l'Abbaye du Bec-Hellouin is a part of one of France's most notable monastic communities. The Abbey of Hellouin was founded in the eleventh century by the knight Herluin and has been an influential center of learning for nearly a thousand years. Since 1948 the Olivetan Benedictine monks have lived at the Abbey with the sisters of Le Bec from the order of St. Frances the Roman. In a mingling of male and female voices that is virtually unique in monastic music, the monks and nuns meet on Sundays and church holidays to celebrate the liturgy. As this recording indicates, the choir's ecumenical repertoire is not limited to Gregorian chant. It includes polyphonic chant in the vernacular, and chant from the Byzantine and Protestant traditions.